FROM
Honky-tonks
TO
HELICOPTERS
Tales of a Rig Medic

FROM Honky-tonks TO HELICOPTERS

Tales of a Rig Medic

Douglas M. Sinclair

The Shetland Times Ltd.
Lerwick
2022

From Honky-tonks to Helicopters – Tales of a Rig Medic

ISBN 978-1-910997-52-9

Front cover image: The author with the semi-submersible oil drilling rig SEDCO 135F anchored in Breiwick, Lerwick. 5th September, 1974. Photo by Dennis Coutts

A catalogue record for this book is available from the British Library.
British Library Cataloguing-in-Publication Data

Printed and Published by
The Shetland Times Ltd.,
Gremista, Lerwick,
Shetland ZE1 0PX.

CONTENTS

PREFACE

It was never my intention to write about my experiences as a medic working on oil rigs but while sorting some photos I came across an album containing those taken at that time. Vivid memories came flooding back of the places visited, the individuals I met and events that occurred while in Texas, on the tow across the Atlantic Ocean, working in the North Sea and back in Lerwick on leave.

My wife, Margaret, was interested when seeing these photos and asked questions as this had been part of my life before we met. After relating several stories she suggested they should be written down – so I made a start, expecting that several hundred words would be all. But, like Topsy, it just grew and grew as one memory triggered another until several thousand words had been written. I jokingly said that my memoir was turning into a book and then thought that perhaps it could be.

I am grateful to The Shetland Times for publishing my work, to Charlotte Black for her encouragement and also Kenneth Shearer for his expertise.

Special thanks to our friend Frances Jamieson for her help and useful suggestions but most of all I would like to thank Margaret for her valued support and assistance.

It is hoped that you, the reader, enjoy these tales and also feel that you have been with me on my journey of a lifetime.

Douglas M. Sinclair

THE SOUTHERN STATES

The southern states with Beaumont, Port Arthur and Miami identified

PORT ARTHUR, TEXAS

Beaumont, Port Arthur, Sabine Pass and surrounding area. *Image: Google Maps*

CHAPTER ONE

SEDCO 135K

HOW IT BEGAN

When I said "but you don't need a passport or visa to go to Shetland" he replied "that's not where you're going, we're flying you out to Texas to join the rig in Port Arthur". He was the manager for SEDCO (South East Drilling Company) in Aberdeen and had just offered me the post of rig medic.

This was the beginning of a once in a lifetime unforgettable experience. It is not everyone who gets the opportunity to be on board a semi-submersible oil drilling rig as it is towed from Texas across the Atlantic Ocean to Scotland.

I was 30 years old and had been working in Aberdeen as a staff nurse at the psychiatric Royal Cornhill Hospital then at the general Aberdeen Royal Infirmary. Following the death of my mother, with whom I had been very close, then the split up with my girlfriend I had decided it was time for a change.

A former colleague who was now working offshore in the North Sea as a rig medic had kept in touch and one day he mentioned that SEDCO was advertising for medics so I said to myself "why no go for it?" After a visit to its office in Aberdeen I submitted an application, was invited to attend for an interview and the rest is history.

It was in June 1973 and with a month's notice behind me the day had come at last. In my room in the Nurses' Home at Foresterhill, Aberdeen, I was busily trying to pack up my clothes plus the "essential equipment" which had been handed to me following my interview. Surprisingly it consisted of a hard hat and a large pair of rubber boots!

This caused a problem as to what piece of luggage could accommodate such bulky articles but I finally settled for my large kit bag.

I left what had been home for over two years and joined my fellow oil rig workers at Aberdeen Airport before commencing our journey to Miami, Florida. This was my first transatlantic flight and it also happened to be in a newly introduced jumbo jet which was both interesting and exciting. On arriving at our destination on 16th June we had to pass through customs and I was confronted by a burly serious looking immigration officer who asked me my name and destination. It was hard to guess what he was thinking when on opening my kit bag he took one look at the rubber boots, shook his head in disbelief and said "just move on." (Incidentally the boots were never needed and were eventually ditched.)

From Miami we flew on a much smaller plane to Beaumont, Texas, a journey of almost three hours. We then transferred to a helicopter for the short flight to Port Arthur which was about 17 miles away. This was to be the first of numerous chopper flights over the next 18 months.

PORT ARTHUR

The heat and humidity hit us. We were taken to a small hotel which had comfortable facilities and was to be our base until we could join the rig, SEDCO 135K, which was nearing completion close by. The hotel had a most welcome outdoor swimming pool in which to relax.

The hotel's swimming pool

Posing in front of the hotel in Port Arthur

With colleagues by the pool

It was fortunate that we had avoided a tornado that had swept through the area just before our arrival but the evidence was there when we saw a completely flattened honky-tonk, i.e. a cheap and disreputable bar where mainly country music is played. Apparently the risk of tornado damage in Port Arthur is higher than both the Texas and US national average.

Somehow we had all arrived in the United States without any dollars, just a few travellers' cheques, and initially had to rely on the toolpusher (rig manager) to cover any expenditure. That evening we gathered in the hotel bar where we were given a free gratis bottle of beer. While enjoying my drink I became aware of the barman using the telephone and at the same time giving furtive looks to us seated oilmen. I thought to myself "aye, aye" and right enough within a quarter of an hour the bar door opened and a number of young and not so young "ladies" entered. My suspicion was confirmed when they joined the tables and asked if we wanted to buy them drinks. Unfortunately for them their requests fell on deaf ears due to our lack of money and they returned to their "business establishment" empty handed and bewildered.

My first impression of Port Arthur was of an extremely flat landscape with a lot of water around and oil related installations. The

The flat landscape around Port Arthur

town is located in Jefferson County, south east Texas, and is adjacent to the Sabine Lake into which the Sabine and Neches Rivers flow. The State of Louisiana borders the east side of the lake. On enquiring I was informed that the town was founded in 1895 and incorporated as a city in 1898. It soon developed into a busy seaport and became a boom town following an oil strike at Spindletop Hill, near Beaumont, on 10th January, 1901. By the mid-20th century Port Arthur had become the biggest oil refining locality in the world.

The town was a combination of a patchwork of different communities which were racially divided. The oil refineries were beyond the residential area. We could not have been sent to south Texas at a worse time as the weather in July reached temperatures of over 90˚F (32˚C), along with high humidity which was oppressive and extremely unpleasant. Consequently salt tablets were supplied and it was important that they were taken.

It was interesting to learn that a Texan tradition is salted beer. Salt was either shaken on the back of a hand and licked or shaken on to the top of a can before drinking while a drinking glass rim was coated with a liquid, or sauce, and then dipped in salt. This was how a drink was served in all beer joints. Some Texans simply sprinkled salt directly into their beer. By the way, later on in oil boom Aberdeen salt cellars were to be found in pubs and often used by, what my fellow oil workers called, the pseudo Texans who frequented the bars – to show off. My colleagues suspected that some of them may have worked on a rig but had never set foot in Texas or ever experienced sweating in really hot, humid weather and it was doubtful if they had understanding of the important role that salt plays in avoiding dehydration.

It was noticeable that nobody in Texas seemed to walk anywhere which I found unusual but never gave it another thought. That was until I went out for a look around and cops in a passing car apprehended me. They must have reckoned I was up to no good as they asked me why I was walking on the road, where had I come from and my destination. The last question couldn't be answered as I hadn't the foggiest idea but was told to return to my accommodation. After that experience I never ventured far out on foot again.

It would seem that there are several reasons for this reluctance to walk, mainly the reliance on cars due to the large distances involved and simply that Americans like driving cars and trucks. There is a negative social pressure on walkers and in particular those who do not use the sidewalk and risk being struck by passing traffic. At that time I couldn't drive so walking everywhere was second nature to me.

Seeing SEDCO 135K for the first time before boarding

JOINING THE RIG

We were soon transferred to the rig but not before the toolpusher asked if I would do him a favour. I could hardly refuse as he was my new boss but to my surprise and dismay the favour was to smuggle his small pet poodle on board in the top of my kit bag which I assumed was an illegal act. My dilemma was if his request was not carried out he could terminate my employment before I even set foot on the rig but on the other hand if caught the consequences were unclear. Anyway, I did as he asked and we passed through security unchallenged and I was more than glad to hand the dog with no name over to him.

He probably chose me because I was the only person with an easily accessible kit bag whereas the others had suitcases. I sincerely hoped

The toolpusher's pet poodle that was smuggled onto the rig

that this would be the first and last time the toolpusher asked me a favour and, as it turned out, it was.

We met our colleagues who had arrived a few weeks before us and they turned out to be the source of useful information. SEDCO 135K had just been constructed by Levingston SB in Orange, a short distance to the northeast of Port Arthur.

After changing into lighter clothing I proceeded to find out what lay ahead. Following a conducted tour of the rig I was informed that my first task was to set up the rig hospital (which was actually just one room, with a small bedroom attached). That entailed identifying and ordering all the appropriate medical equipment, dressings, drugs and stationery required, while at the same time carrying out the work of a rig medic although in a reduced capacity. This was because in

Getting the 135K ready

Chatting with colleagues on board the rig

the advent of a serious accident or emergency any necessary medical intervention would be readily available on shore.

It wasn't long before my title was elevated to that of "Doc".

I was part of a skeleton crew of essential workers that had been specifically flown over to prepare the rig to be operational before it and we were towed across the Atlantic. The crew consisted of the drill team and other key personnel including the electrician, crane operator, radio operator, barge engineer, medic, catering and hotel services' staff including, most importantly, the cooks. Alcohol on the rig was strictly forbidden, as were women as they were thought to bring bad luck.

Access to and from the rig was by means of a personnel transport basket skilfully managed by the crane operator. It was able to transport several of us at one go, however, it took me some time to get used to being jerked up, then left suspended in mid-air, high up over the rig

Observing the personnel transport basket being raised

Equipment waiting to be loaded

before being smoothly and safely landed thanks to the good timing of the crane operator. I initially thought the height might be a problem but this was overcome by simply holding on tightly and directing my gaze into the centre of the basket.

My first contact in the yard was the security officer who also proved to be a valuable source of information. It became apparent that he was keen to find out whether or not I was a member of the Masonic Brethren. I had previously noticed the large number of senior SEDCO staff wearing masonic rings and soon found that the majority of oil workers were indeed masons. After discovering what he wanted to know he proceeded to show me around the construction yard.

One day while walking through the yard he said "see that black m*****f*****? He's a dead man". Shocked by both the language and statement, I was informed that a week or two earlier when this worker was on the rig platform some 60 feet up he had unintentionally kicked a metal bar over the side. It had hit a white colleague below who toppled over into the water and subsequently drowned. Consequently the unfortunate fellow who caused the accident would have to, according to the security officer, constantly keep looking up to make sure nothing fell on his head as his chance of surviving to see the rig completed was slim. Whether he remained alive or not is unknown to me.

With the town being segregated this corresponded to a racial division of labour with the best paying jobs reserved for the white people who lived in the east side of the town. People of colour were employed, mainly for maintenance work, but surprisingly were allowed to join a union. There was almost no oil related work for women.

Naturally life on the rig was not all work and we were allowed time ashore but for me it meant I couldn't go too far away, or for too long,

SEDCO K

being the only medic on board and consequently on call. This was in the days long before mobile phones were in common usage and I wasn't even provided with a pager.

I grabbed every opportunity I could to speak with local people. Generally they were friendly, laid back and somewhat droll individuals but it strongly come across how insular many of them were. Admittedly Texas is a large state but, apart from having knowledge about their own little patch, for the majority of Texans any comprehension of the rest of the state and beyond was non-existent. One told me he had heard of England and that was somewhere in Europe. Another guy inquired where I came from and when I told him he replied that he knew about Shetland ponies but was completely taken aback to discover that Shetland was actually a place. He was interested to discover its location and asked what it was like to live there.

One day we decided to visit the west side of Port Arthur to see what it was like and perhaps have a beer. I mentioned our intended visit to a coloured yard worker whom I had befriended and his response was "if you and I happen to meet there I don't know you." West Port Arthur proved to be an experience. The first person we saw was a cheery individual sitting in a stationary large Cadillac at the side of the road and he was waving and acknowledging all passers-by. Apparently that was his normal behaviour and the car never moved because he didn't have money to buy gasoline. He was also the proud owner of a refrigerator – the only problem was that his home had no electricity.

An even more surprising encounter happened one evening when I was taking a leisurely stroll in the vicinity of the yard while watching and listening to the bullfrogs croaking as it was their mating season. Suddenly an alligator appeared and crossed the track a little distance in front of me. I stopped dead in my tracks but needless to say I didn't stick around.

HONKY-TONKS

Eventually I found myself sitting in a genuine honky-tonk in the east side of Port Arthur. This had become the hangout for the boys who had travelled out earlier. One of them had wasted no time in finding himself a girlfriend who he said worked there – I assumed behind the bar, but not so. On entering we were confronted by a scantily clad go-go dancer who was "performing" in a cage suspended from the ceiling.

We were sitting enjoying a beer when she later came over and I was flabbergasted when she announced "Hey doc, you wanna dance? It'll cost you nothin." The first thing that went through my mind was that it was highly unlikely that I would have paid. I later thought what on earth would folk back home think if they could see me now dancing in a honky-tonk in Texas with a couple of tassels on a bikini top swinging in front of my eyes? We were dancing to Charlie Rich's great hit *Behind Closed Doors* which had just been released.

I had always been passionate about all things American, especially country & western music and also blues and jazz. Port Arthur proved to be heaven as music seemed to emanate from every building in the town. Popular artists over the airwaves were Merle Haggard, Loretta Lynn, George Jones, Tammy Wynette, Conway Twitty, Buck Owens, Charley Pride, Kris Kristofferson and Faron Young whose *It's Four in the Morning* became a classic party favourite. Janis Joplin, another well-known singer, was born in Port Arthur in 1943 but tragically died in 1970. She is probably best remembered for her version of Kris Kristofferson's *Me and Bobby McGee*, (and for her love of Southern Comfort whiskey). Southern Comfort was relatively unknown to me but not so to my colleagues who had frequented the bars before my arrival. They soon introduced me to it but I preferred a Budweiser.

Label from a drink popular with oilmen

Cajun music was also heard as there were several workers who travelled regularly over the bridge from their home in South Louisiana. I was asked by one guy to come and "meet my ol' lady, by the way she's a stripper" but the invitation had to be declined due to the distance involved and the risk of being disciplined or even sacked if there had been an emergency in my absence. However, it was still possible on board the rig to enjoy gumbo, the spicy Creole soup-stew, in addition to the equally popular T-bone steak.

During my short stay in Texas I was able to enjoy playing pool. It was, and probably still is, a favourite American recreational pastime. However, snooker was the popular game when I was young and we regularly played at the Seamen's Mission in Charlotte Street, Lerwick. Although they are both cue games a difference is that pool is played with 16 balls compared with 22 in snooker. While having a game of pool with my mate in a honky-tonk we were approached by two Americans who offered to play doubles. We decided to give it a go and after a hard fought game we had the satisfaction of being the winners. It was only when they suggested we play again but this time for dollars "to make it more interesting" that we realised we had met a couple of chancers and left them to hustle someone else.

Standing by the side of our transport in Port Arthur

One night in the same honky-tonk we had another encounter with Americans. A group of us were sitting around enjoying a beer. One of the boys sitting at my table had moved on to drinking the popular Southern Comfort and had consumed a fair quantity. He was probably having a final blow out before we started the tow as he was well aware that when that happened he wouldn't be able to get another drink for over a month. At one point he staggered up to go to the toilet and bumped into one of the locals sitting at a neighbouring table who immediately threw a punch. Then all hell broke loose. Among the mayhem there he stood in a daze in the middle of the room with the guy next to him swinging a pool cue above his head ready to deliver a blow. I yanked him away to avoid what would probably have been a serious injury that I would have had to deal with. At the same time the sirens were getting louder. The cops arrived and we were all thrown out into the sidewalk. My initial thoughts are unprintable but the excitement at the prospect of ending up in jail was quickly dampened when we were ordered in no uncertain terms to "get back to your rig". We piled into a vehicle driven by one of the drillers who was obviously very drunk but the cops possibly turned a blind eye in their haste to get rid of us. Somehow his driving appeared to be perfectly normal during the short drive back.

After a concentrated effort by everybody the rig was almost ready to leave. My work up to now had involved treating several minor accidents and burns, cuts, splinters, bruises, mosquito bites and such like, but just before the tow commenced I had my first serious emergency. A cook on board one of the river tugs was breaking up ice armed with a pick when his hand slipped and he split his other hand wide open between the ring and middle fingers. With his hand

The crane operator at work

Work continues on rig floor

wrapped in a dish towel he was winched on board the rig for attention. I stabilised his hand using steri-strips, a splint and a bandage. It was a massive relief for me that we had not left as the casualty could be taken off the rig and transferred to a shore hospital for specialised treatment.

THE TOW

It was in mid-July when the tow at last began. With the aid of two river tugs the slow passage commenced through Lake Sabine and then down into Sabine Pass which separates Cameron Parish, Louisiana, on the east side from Jefferson County, Texas, on the west side. The Pass is about four or five nautical miles long and after a short time we entered the Gulf of Mexico.

The local tugs were replaced by an ocean-going German vessel and the tow began in earnest. A member of the tug's crew, whose responsibility it was to manage the tow line, transferred on to the rig for the duration of the tow. He was a knowledgeable guy and we had many interesting conversations.

The tow has begun. Two river tugs are taking the rig down the Sabine Pass to the Gulf of Mexico. Louisiana is on the left and Texas is on the right

Enjoying a break with the crew member from the German tug

As we got further from the shore we passed through the numerous working rigs dotted around, many of which were jack-ups in the relatively shallow water. It was now important that a routine be adopted by everybody to ensure the smooth running and maintenance of the rig. Equally essential was the opportunity to unwind and relax at the end of shifts. Gambling with cards was a favourite pastime in addition to playing pool. I learned the proper way to play poker, but for cents only and not high stakes, and was wondering why I wasn't doing too well until a fellow player enlightened me. At that time I was a smoker and it had become apparent to him that when I had a good hand I smoked faster. That knowledge worked to my advantage as subsequently I was now able to hoodwink my opponents by doing so when I had a poor hand.

A popular card game was "Whores and Fours and One Eyed Jacks" where every queen, four and jack of spades and jack of hearts are wild cards. Another game was "Four Fourteen" where half the pot can be won while having cards totalling four or fourteen but holding an ace and three can ensure the whole pot. It made a change fae playin five hunder!

I was sitting out enjoying the sun one morning when a couple of roustabouts saw me and made a snide comment, suggesting that I was sitting doing nothing while they were doing all the hard work. Rather than ignoring their criticism I surprised them by immediately offering to give them a hand. Part of the work entailed transporting and stacking bags of cement on the drill floor. When still at school in Lerwick and again as a student I had often been employed as a docker, during my holidays, working with the "North Boats" at the Steamers' Store on Victoria Pier. I was also sometimes at Hay & Co., Freefield, unloading cement and wood boats, or working over at the "Gut Factory" at Heogan in Bressay with bags of fish meal. All cargo back then was manhandled using barrows and slings. These experiences gave me a fair idea of what I thought the effort involved would be and that I would be able to safely manage it. My plan paid off as at the end of the shift I had gained their respect - but had also discovered how unfit I really was! I went to bed feeling completely knackered, but reassured that I was accepted as part of the rig team.

On at least one occasion we enjoyed a barbeque on deck. It was great to sit in the balmy evening sun on the wide open space and enjoy our hamburgers and T-bone steaks compared with eating in the cramped rig canteen.

About this time I had an experience that is best forgotten about. Some of my colleagues decided we would go swimming in one of the rig's caisson legs, an exciting prospect at the time and although I was not a strong swimmer it was an opportunity not to be missed. Perched

Enjoying the evening sun. In the foreground is the personnel transport basket

The barbeque is under way on the deck in the Gulf of Mexico

on a ledge I launched myself with the intention of swimming across the cavity to reach a similar ledge on the other side. Halfway across I panicked when the realisation hit me that I was in deep sea water and not in a regular swimming pool. I felt myself going under. My next recollection was being hauled out by two guys. Needless to say that was my first and last swimming venture in a caisson.

After leaving the Gulf of Mexico we passed the Florida Keys then entered the Straits of Florida and the Atlantic Ocean. One evening, about 10 days after leaving Port Arthur, we were entertained by a spectacular display of the colourful neon lights of Miami shining through the darkness in the distance as we continued on our journey north along the coast. After some days a course was set to the north east and the United States faded away into the distance. That was the last time land was seen for several weeks.

To avoid accidents the decision was made that strenuous or what could be termed dangerous work should not be undertaken as we were now getting further and further from land. However, a potential emergency did arise. One of the crew presented with severe abdominal pain and discomfort. Before I had time to assess the situation the toolpusher diagnosed acute appendicitis, was adamant that he was correct and to my horror asked “you gonna operate doc?” I dismissed his suggestion and uttered the words that anyone who has ever been hospitalised has been asked, namely “has your bowels moved”? It transpired that the patient had been one of the earlier workers to be flown out and with the heat and humidity I suspected that he could be suffering from constipation. My suspicion was confirmed and the only treatment he needed was an enema. The procedure proved to be a great success - and a great relief for me. If the decision had been made to call out the American Coastguard for a misdiagnosis, with the expense involved, my days as a rig medic would no doubt have been over. Thankfully that was the only hairy moment during the Atlantic crossing.

The Atlantic can be a lonely place but there was always something to watch such as flying fish skimming over the surface and the beautiful sunrises and sunsets. I had hoped to see the green flash, the meteorological optical phenomena where, for a few seconds, a distinct green spot can be seen above the upper rim of the sun at sunrise and sunset if the conditions are right. Unfortunately I never once saw it - perhaps the conditions were never right or I simply blinked and missed it!

The isolation was interrupted by the sight of an occasional ship ploughing its way often through choppy conditions. The days passed quickly due to work and the company of others.

Soon we were aware of land in the distance and eventually we reached Falmouth, Cornwall, at the end of August. After a brief stop we carried on through the English Channel and into the North Sea then to the Firth of Forth to Aberlady Bay, East Lothian, which was our final destination. (The rig was then provisioned and later left to drill the first test well for the BP-Ranger consortium 100 miles north east of Shetland.)

My time on SEDCO 135K was over and I came ashore on leave along with others and we were transported to Aberdeen where we had been appointed. I was responsible for making my own travel arrangements to Shetland where my father and sister Dorothy were waiting to meet me at Sumburgh Airport. They hurried straight past me and got a shock when I said “ir you no spaekin?” I was apparently unrecognisable with my new gear, tanned skin, hair longer than ever before and moustache. Dorothy turned, took one look and said “I towt du wis a Mexican”.

CHAPTER TWO

SEDCO 135F

BACK TO WORK

After time in Lerwick I went back to Aberdeen to begin my first stint on SEDCO 135F which was also a three-legged semi-submersible oil drilling rig. This was in mid-September 1973. The reason I could not return to SEDCO 135K was because the dual role of radio operator/ medic was now required rather than just a medic.

As I had originally been appointed in Aberdeen I still had to crew change from there. The rig was slightly older than SEDCO 135K having been built in 1967 by Victoria MD in Victoria, British Columbia, Canada. In 1971 it had been towed 16,000 miles on a 160 day journey from where it had been working in New Zealand waters to drill in the Norwegian Sector of the North Sea. It was said to have been the longest tow ever undertaken, the most difficult, the most expensive and the German tug was the largest and most powerful in the world. When I joined the rig it had relocated to the UK sector and was drilling for oil to the north east of Shetland.

After my first North Sea helicopter flight which was in a Bristow Sikorsky S61, and having removed my immersion suit, I stepped on to the rig. Waiting for me to relieve him was my opposite number who gave me a handover report. I was once again the only medic on board and on 24-hour call. Immediately I felt that it was a completely different environment compared with before. This was an operational rig which was drilling for oil at full steam ahead with a crew complement of about 65 of which 50 had been hired in Aberdeen. I discovered some men were Aberdonians while others were from

A Bristow Sikorsky S61 leaving the rig

different areas of Scotland and England. Most, but not all, were working 12 hour shifts.

My next move was to familiarise myself with the general layout of the rig followed by an inspection of the hospital and its contents. When investigating the facilities for the storage of drugs I found that the locked cupboard designated for "Controlled Drugs" only contained vitamins. A search of the main drug cabinet revealed that the controlled drugs were kept there and to my amazement and concern the labels were written in Norwegian, obviously from when the rig was operating in the Norwegian sector. (The controlled drugs usually kept on board rigs were opiates such as morphine, diamorphine and dihydrocodeine, all given to alleviate severe pain.) This raised the question as to the level of in-depth knowledge and experience possessed by previous medics and also reinforced the opinion often expressed by some American rig managers that employing highly skilled medical personnel was not necessary. These men were used to working in the Gulf of Mexico where there was quick and easy access to medical assistance on shore and they seemed to be totally unaware of the distances involved in the North Sea and the harsh and demanding conditions. At that time not all medics were registered nurses who were accustomed to the strict NHS regulations regarding the storage and administration of these drugs.

ROLES

I soon found out what multi-tasking meant. My work involved attending to any medical emergencies, providing a daily surgery, which often included a counselling role, completing a daily medical log record and participating with other colleagues to ensure that occupational health and safety regulations were being adhered to. I was also responsible for mail deliveries, drawing up crew change lists and liaising with chopper pilots on the helideck, also organising medical evacuations (medevacs) when a worker had to be airlifted for treatment on shore. I had access to an onshore doctor and the rig toolpusher who was my line manager. The rig hospital and my small bedroom were situated next to the recreation room where staff could relax, discuss any issues, play cards or darts and also watch movies. Another of my duties was to screen these at certain times depending on shift duties. There were no DVDs back then, the films were sent out and I had to manually operate a reel to reel projector.

It was interesting to discover exactly what the roles were of all the individuals involved with the rig. Some were self-explanatory such as cook, steward and radio operator, while other duties were exclusively linked to working in the oil industry, e.g. the barge engineer. He was responsible for marine matters such as navigation, anchor handling, stability, loading and unloading, weight distribution and relevant maintenance work. There were also geologists, whose job was to analyse, evaluate and describe rock formations while drilling, and welders who operated, maintained and repaired all types of equipment used when drilling and were specialised in high-pressure and high temperature welding. Electricians oversaw the commissioning and provided maintenance follow up and repair for all electrical equipment including drilling.

On the drill deck the toolpusher provided leadership for the drill team members. Next in line was the driller who was in charge of the well drilling process and also the supervision of the crew. Another duty entailed monitoring pressure build-up and gas levels. The assistant driller supervised the work on the drill floor also drilling

SEDCO 135F drilling for Amoco

operations. He was also responsible for the motormen who performed maintenance, daily inspections of equipment and small repairs to drilling equipment. The derrickman at the top of the derrick guided the drill pipe into the drill hole and was also in charge of the mud-processing area. Mud is used to lubricate and cool the drill bit and carry rock cuttings to the surface.

The crane operator was responsible for setting up cranes and operating them by moving material around the site while monitoring crane stability and load weight. He was also in charge of conducting machine safety checks each day and ensuring site safety.

Roughnecks worked under the direction of the driller to make or break connections as the drill pipe was tripped in or out of the hole, also for maintaining and repairing much of the equipment found

The crane operator

on the drill floor and derrick. Roustabouts were managed by the crane operator and they assisted the drilling team. Duties included maintaining equipment, unloading supplies and cleaning, scraping and painting the deck, equipment and work areas.

This is in contrast to lead hands who were unskilled labourers whose main duty was to assist other crew members and to clean up each day.

The rig personnel were a motley bunch of different nationalities but the majority of senior staff were Americans. Most crew members were British as SEDCO's standard practice was to recruit local labour as it was cheaper. It seemed that others originated from areas where the rig had previously been working, e.g. the barge engineer was Australian while one of the toolpushers was Canadian. It was with him that I committed a major faux pas when enquiring what part of Texas he came from - that didn't go down well. SEDCO 135F appeared to be a trouble free "happy ship". The only staff incident I can recall took place in the rig galley when a member of the catering team received a broken nose during an altercation with the cook and had to receive treatment.

CREW CHANGES

This could be a revelation because you never knew from one crew change to the next who would turn up on the rig. One day the chopper pilot called me over to deal with a new arrival. On board was a poor fellow sitting frozen to the seat unable to move. With help he was assisted to the hospital where on questioning the man replied that when looking out the window he was suddenly aware of how high up it was from the sea and became frightened. He confessed to being scared of heights and suffered from vertigo. After some time I suggested we go on the rig deck to get some fresh air to help him relax. This was an extremely bad move on my part because when we got there he went across to look over the railing and it all happened again. A couple of roustabouts helped me to carry him into the hospital. After receiving medication to relieve his anxiety he finally admitted that it had never been his intention of ever joining the crew but had come for a look as he had always wondered what it was like to be on an oil rig. Not surprisingly his name was added to the next crew change manifest.

On another occasion a guy arrived to work as a steward in the catering department. He seemed vaguely familiar but it took me a day or two before remembering that he had been a patient in the psychiatric hospital in Aberdeen where I had previously worked. It transpired that he had also recognised me and it soon became apparent that he was greatly concerned that his line manager would be informed of his previous hospital admission. I informed him that this would not be the case as he was perfectly capable of carrying out his duties but, unconvinced, he only lasted the one trip and never returned.

Most crew changes were straight forward but the next encounter with a new employee turned out to be a pretty kettle of fish, to use a saying frequently used by the Americans. A new lead hand arrived and, once again, he looked familiar then I remembered him as also having been a patient in the psychiatric hospital. However, it was in a secure unit where he had been sectioned, i.e. kept in hospital under the Mental Health Act. This was because he had carried out an act of arson by setting fire to a Christmas tree in Union Street, Aberdeen. On

A break from work

this occasion it was necessary to inform the toolpusher and on hearing the details he almost had a heart attack. In fact a Christmas tree on an oil rig is the name given to a piece of heavy equipment that controls the flow produced by a well. An arsonist was the last person anyone wanted on board, especially one connected with a Christmas tree. An instruction was immediately issued that a seat be reserved for him on the next available chopper.

During my time working offshore the one thing that caused me much inconvenience and expense was the rule strictly adhered to by SEDCO that identified your home base as the place where you had been recruited. Unfortunately for me that was Aberdeen and therefore every crew change originated from there and not Shetland. I had to make own way to Lerwick every leave and back to Aberdeen at my own expense.

Eventually I thought I had partially solved the problem after asking the chopper pilot if there was any chance that he could take a detour to Shetland on his way to Aberdeen and drop me off at Sumburgh Airport. He said "sure, no problem, I can refuel there". This meant that I got home quicker and only had to travel to Aberdeen at the end of my leave to join the rig. All went well for several trips until the inevitable happened. Apparently soon after had I left the chopper at Sumburgh it broke down and the pilot announced that "if it hadn't been for dropping off that medic we would now be in Aberdeen". I was totally unaware of this until I was met with a frosty reception on arriving at Dyce for the next crew change. From then on every time I spoke with the pilot on the helideck I was aware that there were always roustabouts within earshot. They were making sure that there would never again be a refuelling stop in Sumburgh. There wasn't.

THE DIVERS

Key personnel on board were the divers whose tasks included identifying faults and weaknesses in the rig structure, carrying out repairs and also general maintenance. I got to know them well as they regularly came to the recreation room to relax. We often chatted and consequently became close friends. After one crew change I stepped on to the rig and could sense that things were not quite right as there was a change of atmosphere. My opposite rig medic briefed me before he made his way to the helideck. It turned out that one of the young divers had undertaken a routine dive in a bell without difficulty but on commencing decompression in the chamber on board the rig he had become unwell and experienced chest pain. (The chamber was a small room that allowed divers at the end of a dive to complete their decompression stops on the rig rather than underwater. Divers were exposed to lower amounts of air pressure until normal air pressure was reached). He remained in the decompression chamber and several times had to be recompressed i.e. to higher pressure, which relieved the pain, but when decompressed the pain returned.

When his condition hadn't improved medical assistance was requested and a doctor and an expert diver arrived on the rig. The doctor diagnosed pleurisy and pneumonia of the left lung and prescribed an antibiotic and instructed that decompression be continued so that the diver could then be airlifted to hospital. All the divers disagreed with the diagnosis as they were positive that the problem was a pneumothorax, i.e. the presence of air or gas in the cavity between the lungs and the chest wall, causing potential collapse of the lung. The advice from the expert diver was that the diver should continue to be re-compressed and decompressed over a period of days or even weeks. However, their hands were tied as they could not argue with a doctor who, against their wishes, had left the rig. When the diver's condition deteriorated the doctor was called back. He undertook a brief examination and then actually told the diver to pull himself together although he was showing some disorientation, distress and restlessness. Pain killers, tranquilisers and sleeping tablets were then administered which caused the divers great concern as they knew this to be the wrong course of action.

The following day the diver's lungs collapsed and he died. This was the situation I walked into. Understandably feelings among the divers were running high and the doctor had to be protected while waiting to be airlifted ashore as they were threatening to hang him from the derrick. I now faced the most harrowing few hours of my time on the rigs because as medic I had to assist in retrieving the deceased whom I had known well. This tragedy obviously affected everybody and created a somewhat sombre atmosphere throughout the rig.

Later that year an enquiry into the incident exonerated both the diving company KD Marine and SEDCO. The doctor, however, was found to have caused the death by misdiagnosing and administering totally inappropriate drugs. It transpired he had never attended any course on decompression or had knowledge of diving accidents.

On a lighter note, before the tragedy occurred, I had actually been in the decompression chamber. The pressure was increased until I experienced the phenomenon of my voice strangely sounding like Donald Duck which was caused by the helium content of the gas mixture in the chamber affecting my vocal chords and changing voice sounds. Although humorous this was actually a serious exercise. It was important that I was familiar with the procedure and it was undertaken to discover how I would cope both mentally and physically with being confined in the decompression chamber. Thankfully I had no feeling of claustrophobia, perhaps because everything that took place was so interesting, and therefore I would not have felt apprehensive if called to attend a diving emergency. It was a relief that this situation never arose.

DAILY ROUTINE

Every day I held what was known as a surgery. This provided everyone on the rig with the opportunity to visit the hospital to receive either treatment or advice for whatever was concerning them. It turned out to be a widespread and diverse amount of issues. Most who attended had comparatively minor ailments such as knocks, cuts, bruises, burns, strains, sprains, skin rashes, indigestion or even headaches. Eye related problems were common among oil rig workers as the constant presence of wind often caused dryness. Very often it was either just dust or specks of dirt in the eye that could be flushed out with water and eye wash stations were readily available. More serious was welder's flash or arc eye. Although welders wore protection and knew the dangers, other workers sometimes did not realise that they were in the vicinity of welding taking place and that the cornea of their unprotected eyes could be flash burned. This is similar to sunburn causing intense pain in the affected eye or eyes but usually with treatment heals within a day or two. The crew were regularly reminded to keep their distance when welding was being undertaken. Thankfully serious incidents were rare and, if any occurred, a medevac was arranged in consultation with the shore doctor to either Aberdeen or Shetland.

There were often individuals who requested a shot of penicillin as they had somehow contracted venereal disease. Their request was refused and they were advised to attend the Special Clinic which at that time was at Woolmanhill in Aberdeen. One guy on his return to work thanked me very much for my advice as his visit to the clinic had solved his problem. Unfortunately his wife was still not speaking to him.

My psychiatric training proved to be useful as I was very often able to pick up psychological and mental health issues. Armed with this information in many cases it was simply a matter of listening to the person's concerns and providing support and reassurance, or offering advice on where they could obtain specialist help.

HOME LEAVE

"All work and no play make Jack a dull boy" is a well-known proverb and after two intense weeks on the rig home leave was a welcome distraction. During the years I had worked in Aberdeen it was not always possible to get back for Up-Helly-A' and as a result my place in the "Soond Boys" squad had been relinquished. While at home and yarning with a neighbour, John Abernethy, he asked if I would like to come out in "his squad" and as luck would have it the date of the festival worked out with my shift pattern. The squad had previously been connected with the Grand Hotel but was now with The Lounge Bar. However, squad meetings continued to be held in a cellar under the bar in the Grand Hotel and I attended whenever I was home. Teacher Maurice Manson was the Guizer Jarl that year. The squad name was "Heath's Cod Ends" which was based on the so called Cod War between Iceland and the UK over fishing limits during Ted Heath's time as Prime Minister. The skit involved several props including a large net and a number of cardboard cod. As the night wore on many of the squad became more and more drunk until by the time we visited the last hall there were not enough of us in a fit state to undertake the net tug of war. John later pronounced "you're aa just a bunch o' drunken little bu****s" and he never let us forget it.

This was the squad I remained with until 2006 which was the last year I participated in Up-Helly-A'.

During another spell at home my cousin Ertie Fullerton asked if I would like to join him on his boat and take part in an all-night fishing competition. Naturally I jumped at the chance and we set off from Scalloway to fish on the west side but had mixed fortunes. He caught nothing and I had limited success. We gave up due to increasing wind and swell and anchored off Oxna all night. In the morning we attended the weigh-in to find that few boats had participated or, like us, had

Up-Helly-Aa' 1974. Squad 21 Heath's Cod Ends. *Photo by Dennis Coutts*

Back row (from left): William Jamieson, Douglas Sinclair, John Firth, Ian Byrne, John Henderson, Hunter Jamieson, John Anderson, Bobby Peterson (Patter) and Jacky Tait. Middle row: American Musician, John MacRae, Robbie Pearson, James Leask, John Abernethy, Andrew Williamson and Andrew Jamieson. Front row: Nigel Miller, Michael Gray, David Malcolmson, George Miller, David Blance and Philip Manson.

abandoned fishing due to the weather. Lerwick man John Hoseason had caught a skate off Lunning and was declared the winner. I was surprised to discover that I was the runner up and was more than slightly embarrassed to be awarded a shield for my catch – two peerie olicks (small ling).

My salary as a rig medic was considerably more than that of a staff nurse with Grampian Health Board and this enabled me to add to my collection of old Shetland books. I had inherited my great aunt's postcards and books but was always keen to buy some more. Responding to the "For Sale" adverts in *The Shetland Times* and placing the occasional "Wanted" request was often fruitful.

Harry Hay's saleroom became a favourite haunt. His auction room was upstairs in a building in Mounthooly Street, now demolished. This was adjacent to where Da Steak Hoose is now. Many Lerwick ladies sat there with their knitting during the sales which took place on Wednesday afternoons and sometimes the evenings. Any punter who was standing at the back on the occasion when the floor gave way and the sofas sank down causing the ladies' legs to fly up in the air will never forget the sight!

At that time Norwegian clasp cardigans/jackets were on-trend, to use a current term, and Syversens' clothing and wool shop at 125-127 Commercial Street was the supplier. Needless to say I bought one and when a guy offshore saw me wearing it he asked if I could get him something similar. Sverre Syversen, or Steve as he liked to be called, saw a business opportunity and asked me if I would be prepared to sell these on his behalf. A selection was made ready for me to take every time I returned to the rig and this proved to be a great success as they sold like hot cakes. For doing him a favour I was given an unusual patterned example as a gift.

Sverre was a Norwegian who was a crew member on an MTB, (motor torpedo boat), that was based in Lerwick during the Second World War. He returned to marry and eventually settled in Lerwick where he opened a butcher shop called Lerwick Meat Company in the main part of what is now the British Red Cross shop at 125-127 Commercial Street. He and his wife later opened Syversens' in the same premises which had been extended to include the part next to Reform Lane. Some years later they moved to the Aberdeen area.

THE THREE Ps

During my time off I always found something to do and somewhere to go. It was often said that for some the main evening entertainment

National Commonwealth Day 1959 is being celebrated at the North Star Cinema, with commissionaire Tammy Duncan and manager Alex Greig at the entrance. The film "Behind the Mask" was released in October the previous year. *Photo courtesy of Tammy Duncan jnr*

in Lerwick at that time was the three Ps, namely "da picters, Planets an pubs" and I frequented them all. "Da picters" was the North Star cinema in Harbour Street but by the early 1970s it was past its heyday. Back in the 1950s and 60s queues often stretched up the street and around the corner and along Market Street with people waiting to see blockbusters.

Who could ever forget sitting in the "scratchers", (the front stalls), and being engulfed by Cromessol Fragrant Disinfectant being liberally sprayed as a public health measure by the cinema commissionaire, Tammy Duncan, resplendent in his braided uniform.

Another unforgettable event was the evening when someone sitting near me in the stalls farted and it was so loud that the courting couples who were in the back row of the balcony heard the explosion. The resulting laughter that reverberated throughout the whole building was unremitting and as a result the film was paused. The usherettes appeared with their torches flashing in an attempt to discover the culprit but it was a fruitless search as he kept his head down and remained silent. The main lights had to be switched on and eventually calm was restored and the film resumed.

Some unwelcome furry visitors to the North Star were the rats from the slaughterhouse which was situated opposite. In some areas of the cinema one had to be careful, when retrieving anything that had fallen on the floor, to avoid accidently setting off a rat trap. On Sundays Tammy along with chief projectionist Jock Sutherland inspected the building and disposed of the vermin.

The cinema was so popular that regulars had "dir ain saets" and woe betide anyone who inadvertently occupied them. They were stood over and stared at until they got the message and moved. Cinema goers had to endure sitting in the clouds of cigarette smoke that permeated the stalls. Very often it was not only the smoke that was annoying but also the unpleasant odour from Russian cigarettes that that been illicitly acquired from the crews of the vessels frequenting Lerwick at that time. These were water carriers supplying the Russian fleet that was fishing around Shetland.

The North Star closed as a cinema in 1989 and became a nightclub until 2007. It was a sad day in September 2011 when the building was demolished.

The Planets Ballroom in Mounthooly Street, now Chapel House, has special memories for me as when I was in my late teens I was a member of the Midniters, the popular band that regularly played there. The musicians were Arnie Arcus, lead guitar, Jackie Sinclair, rhythm guitar, Sidney Hunter, bass guitar, his brother Stanley on accordion, Bobby Ganson, drums, and me on the piano. We played a wide range of music for jive, ballroom and Scottish dancing, ending with appropriate songs for smooching under the mirror or glitter ball. Cliff Richard and The Shadows were popular at the time and several of their tunes and songs were covered including *Apache, Living Doll* and *The Young Ones*. Others were *Walk don't Run* by the Ventures; *Bye Bye Love* and *Be Bop-A-Lula*, by the Everly Brothers; *Little Runaway* by Del Shannon; *Lonely Boy* by Paul Anka and *Oh Carol* by Neil Sedaka, to name but a few.

As alcohol wasn't allowed in the building "kerry oots" in brown paper bags, bought from the pubs, were handed over at the cloakroom to be retrieved at the end of the evening before heading off to a party somewhere. Bags were often hidden in nearby gardens in the Heddell's Park housing scheme. Women's handbags were inspected too so it was impossible to sneak alcohol into the Planets. It was an extremely well managed dancehall even when there were altercations with visiting fishermen and Royal Navy sailors. I remember one evening watching police eject rowdy fishermen from the Planets then manhandle them

The Midniters. Back row (from left): Jackie Sinclair, Arnie Arcus and Sidney Hunter. Front row: Stanley Hunter, Bobby Ganson and Douglas Sinclair

into the back of the Black Maria (the police van). However, the police were too preoccupied to notice that some managed to escape by the front passenger door and make their way down the street.

With much sadness the dancehall closed in 1976 to become a licensed restaurant with function provision.

My regular pub was The Lounge, with publican Hughie Robertson assisted by his wife Jemima. I was probably there for more hours than was healthy but it was relaxing to catch up with the boys in the public bar for a pint, have a game of five hunder or play darts or dominoes. The impromptu music sessions upstairs in the lounge bar by both local and visiting musicians, some famous and some not so famous, drew in the crowds – as they still do. It would be impossible to write about The Lounge without mentioning regular virtuoso guitar player "Peerie" Willie Johnson and expert pianist John (Bogie) Dalziel.

The pub was perhaps too convenient as I lived in nearby Chapel Place with my father, sister Laurna, brother-in-law Kenny Grant and their young son John. Many years later John trained to become a pilot and for a time flew helicopters to and from the oil rigs and platforms; he is now with HM Coastguard Search and Rescue (SAR) based at Sumburgh.

With the extra money in my pocket plus the spare time, it was easy to over indulge and spend the next day feeling miserable and vowing that "alcohol will never pass my lips again". Famous last words! This situation was shared by other offshore workers. Inevitably there is a down side. For many the frequent abuse of alcohol resulted in the development of mental health issues and also friendship and marital breakdowns.

On returning to the rig following leave I often had individuals visiting the hospital pleading for medication to alleviate the side effects of alcohol withdrawal. That gave me the opportunity to highlight the risks associated with their pattern of drinking and provide advice about reducing the amount they drank. One guy suffering from delirium tremens told me he had been tormented all night by seeing snakes crawling under his bedroom door. Unfortunately my advice to him obviously fell on deaf ears as on the next crew change he was back again in the same sorry state.

STANDBY AND SUPPLY VESSELS

Oil rigs are supported by standby rescue vessels and offshore supply vessels. In 1965 when the jack-up rig Sea Gem was preparing to be moved to another site off the coast of Lincolnshire it collapsed and sank with the loss of 13 men. Following the disaster the need

Standby and supply vessels

for a dedicated rescue vessel to remain in constant attendance was identified. The standby vessels were converted side trawlers and were perfect for operating in what could be harsh conditions in the North Sea. Consequently the crew consisted mostly of retired trawlermen who were ideally suited for the work as they were used to severe weather conditions and being at sea for several weeks at a time. Although skilled seamen, their insufficient knowledge of medical conditions and first aid became apparent to me when a crew member on a standby vessel with an injured knee was winched on board the rig for treatment. I must admit I was taken aback when I removed the bandage to discover that an aspirin had been applied to the injured area in an attempt to alleviate pain!

The supply boats play an important role in the safety and efficiency of oil installations. They literally transport everything required from food to materials and equipment between the supply base and installations. In addition they undertake anchor handling, towing and firefighting operations.

I remember receiving a call from the skipper of a supply boat that was alongside the rig requesting me to come on-board to provide medical treatment for a crew member. He had been struck on the head by a hook while working with a heavy load on deck. Armed with a medical pack I was lowered down by basket to the vessel by crane from the rig. However, it was only when on the deck that I was aware of how much the vessel was heaving up and down due to the swell. I pride myself with having what is termed sea legs but the motion was the like of which I had never experienced before and found it almost impossible to stand throughout my time on board. With a great deal of difficulty I managed to reach the cabin where the injured man was lying in a bunk but the vessel was so unsteady I had to treat him while sitting down. As he had received a nasty head injury a medevac to hospital was necessary. In my opinion he was not in an ambulant state and was therefore tentatively hoisted up by crane on a stretcher, supported by me, on to the rig. The casualty was then taken by chopper to Aberdeen Royal Infirmary.

I was glad to have my feet firmly back on the rig and don't envy those who work on any small vessel in the North Sea during stormy weather – they have my admiration.

Although I organised many medevacs I was only actively involved in one. I was sleeping when wakened at 3am by frantic knocking on my door and shouts for the medic. I rushed to the drill floor to find that a large wire had snapped and swept across the deck injuring one of the drillers. He had sustained a bad compound fracture of the humerus, i.e. the bone in the upper arm. I became worried by his reaction to the accident as I would have expected him to have shown symptoms of shock, but instead he appeared totally unconcerned. Following consultation with a doctor arrangements were made for his transfer to Shetland and for me to accompany him. With his injured arm well supported we had an uneventful trip and on reaching Lerwick the casualty was handed over to staff at the Gilbert Bain Hospital who were somewhat surprised but delighted to see me. I then returned to the rig however while on the journey there I suddenly became alarmed when the chopper dropped like a stone leaving my stomach in my mouth and wondering if we were ditching. I discovered that the pilot had seized an opportunity to buzz a Russian submarine. It certainly was an experience I would rather not repeat.

J.J.

My one and only experience on a supply boat brought home the volatility of the North Sea. During my time offshore there were indeed frequent storms and bad weather. When working one day in the hospital I became aware that the rig had an unusual movement and on glancing over to the window I saw a large wave passing by. It suddenly struck me that before it could be seen from where I was standing it had to be at least 60 feet high. If only I had taken a photo ...

On another occasion when the rig was drilling 100 miles east of Lerwick the toolpusher, always referred to as J.J., informed me that an installation had sunk in an area not far from us, a caisson leg had broken off and was heading in our direction. He requested that I compile an evacuation list and also include the names of essential personnel to remain on board. On handing over the list J.J. proceeded to inform me that a name was missing from the essential personnel part of the list and said "that's you. I need you to look after me and the cook to give me somethin to eat and if this lil ol' rig goes down you'll be the two guys along with me". I thought he was joking then foolishly enquired that if the leg should hit the rig how would we get off. He replied "we don't". Thankfully it passed by, the rig wasn't evacuated and my potential demise was avoided.

I normally worked on the same shift as J.J. and he was a larger than life Texan in more ways than one as he was hefty and somewhat overweight. Nobody knew what his Christian names were until the day a letter arrived addressed to him and all was revealed. On handing it over he said "boy – keep your mouth shut" and I immediately got the message. His names were Julius Joyce.

His sense of humour was very similar to that of many Shetlanders, including myself. His somewhat outlandish and often vulgar turn of phrase and sayings were great but most were unrepeatable. A good example was when I attempted to teach him how to play darts. The game was popular with members of the British crew but seemed to be alien to the Americans on board. We soon got a game underway and J.J. tried his best but I was well ahead and at the stage where I was able to say "see that little space under the 20 at the top of the board, that's called double top. If I hit there with one dart that's 40 points and then the game will be over". He replied "boy, if you hit that with one dart I'll kiss your ass till my nose bleeds". With the first dart I hit the spot and turning to him said "J.J. – start kissing". He laughed but that was his first and last game of darts with me.

MORE TEXANS

I got to know many of the crew when relaxing in the recreation room during our off duty times. The food on the rig could not be faulted and catered for all tastes. Our American colleagues were particularly fond of their grub and plenty of it. This was highlighted when I was accosted by an irate assistant cook, who was spitting fire. He informed me that a guy had asked for a sixteen egg omelette for his breakfast but he had given the greedy so and so four as he reckoned that was more than sufficient. I wondered if "the glutton" was the same enormous guy I had seen the day before with two large T-bone steaks on his plate along with all the trimmings. This particular assistant cook must have been off duty at the time.

During a conversation with a Texan he said in passing that I would know the guy he sat next to at school. What went through my mind was "hoo da hell wid I ken wha sat wi him at school?" To my astonishment it turned out to be Roy Orbison, the famous singer remembered for his hits such as *Pretty Woman* and *Crying* also his time with the Traveling Wilburys. Back then he was one of my favourite musicians and still is. I was so taken aback that I omitted to ask if they had kept in touch which was a pity as it would have been interesting to learn more about him from someone who actually knew him.

THE BIRDS

During my whole rig experience there is one occurrence I will never forget – it happened on the night that natural gas was being burned off. This was a controlled burning to stabilise pressure and flow from

Burning off gas on SEDCO 135F

A supply boat leaving the rig

The hard hat identifies Medic Doug Sinclair

the oil well. As darkness fell hundreds of land, sea and migratory birds started to gather, attracted by the light and heat of the flare. They kept arriving and from the top of the derrick and down to the surface of the sea they continued to circle the rig all night long and created a noise which added to the rumbling from the flare stack. There were birds of all species large and small as well as common and rare including, quite unexpectedly, a snowy owl.

Next morning the heartbreaking sight met us of a number of dead birds both floating in the sea and strewn over the deck. Many had become disoriented and collided with the rig while others who were migrants had collapsed due to exhaustion. Some were incinerated due to overexposure to the heat from the flare.

Apparently the effect of nocturnal attraction of birds to a flare stack can be exacerbated by low cloud cover, fog, precipitation or simply the number of birds in the vicinity.

A WELCOME BREAK

After arriving in Aberdeen following a crew change in August, I went for a pint with Alfie. He was a fellow crewman on the rig with whom I had become friendly and I was filling in time before travelling back to Shetland. During a conversation we came to the conclusion that it would be great to have a short break somewhere in the sun. On leaving the pub we went straight to a travel agent and asked if there was a holiday package immediately available to any destination from Aberdeen. The next day we found ourselves in a hotel in Puerto de la Cruz on the north side of Tenerife. In the evening, after a very pleasant day familiarising ourselves with the town, we went for dinner. We had bought a phrasebook and like many others before us decided to have a go and Alfie proceeded to order our meals in Spanish. When the waiter returned with another waiter instead of two plates of food we were made aware of our lack of linguistic skills and he decided to stick with English, or Doric to be accurate, for the rest of the holiday.

The peace and quiet of the town was a contrast to the noise, hustle and bustle on the rig. Puerto de la Cruz is famous for being the first tourist destination in the world as its warm climate and picturesque setting attracted visitors. We found it to be a very friendly place and not commercialised. There were hotels, cafes and bars interspersed

On holiday with Alfie in Puerto de la Cruz, Tenerife

with residential areas, schools, small banana plantations and a lido bordering the black sandy beach. When our week was up we left our sun umbrellas with some lasses we had met and set off for Aberdeen and I carried on to Shetland for the remainder of my leave.

Coming down the Sound Brae on Leask's bus on my way to Lerwick I saw "my rig" SEDCO 135F anchored in Breiwick. She had come in for a survey and was the third to visit as SEDCO 135G and SEDCO 135R had been in during the previous month for the same purpose. As oil exploration in the North Sea was still at an early stage these rigs were a novelty and a big attraction as for most folk it was the first time that they had seen a semi-submersible rig.

Photographer Dennis Coutts discovered that I was home and, always ready with his camera, took a photo of me sitting on the gunnel of a boat at the Sea Road with the rig and the Wart of Bressay in the background. I found myself featured in the next edition of *The Shetland Times*.

For me it was somewhat strange to walk around the crowded Knab and see the rig there. Several people stopped to have a yarn and some knew I worked on board while others didn't and were amazed. Many will remember being at the Knab and listening to country music wafting across from the oil installations that anchored in Breiwick from time to time.

It would have been so easy to have gone by boat to the rig and been hoisted on board at the end of my leave but, no, I had to go to Aberdeen to undertake the crew change and come all the way back by chopper to be landed on the rig in Breiwick. As far as I was concerned it was a complete waste of time and money. However, when thinking back and remembering the many interesting places and views I had seen since I became a rig medic, it was a surreal experience to look out the rig's hospital window and instead of seeing a vast open expanse of sea what lay before me was the lights of Lerwick.

A day or so later we were under tow again and I remember watching the Ness of Sound disappearing as we headed towards the point of the Bard and out to explore and drill at another site.

TIME FOR A CHANGE

Although my work as a rig medic was enjoyable, as was the way of life on the rig where I had made many good friends, the constant travelling and overnight stays in Aberdeen before each trip offshore was frustrating, tiring and costly. In addition I was unable to join or participate in the various local organisations and activities that interested me due to the limited time spent at home.

The semi-submersible oil drilling rig SEDCO 135F anchored in Breiwick with me in the foreground. 5th September, 1974. *Photo by Dennis Coutts*

What was noticeable during the time I travelled back and forth through Sumburgh Airport was the increasing number of fixed wing and helicopter movements with ever expanding passenger numbers. Most crew changes were now operating via Sumburgh to the East Shetland Basin. The Virkie Terminal seemed to be always bursting at the seams and both it and air traffic at the airport was incredibly busy contrasting with just two or three years earlier when there were only a small number of scheduled flights. It was nearly almost out of the question to find somewhere to sit while waiting for departure and any flight delays caused the situation to become nigh impossible. Any available space was occupied by oil workers who had resorted to sitting on their large holdalls.

Things came to a head when I happened to say to a friend "wirkin on a rig is laek bein on a treadmill". That gave me a shock and set me thinking about my future as up until that day I hadn't considered leaving. The constant travelling was an inconvenience along with winter and its stormy weather. On reflection if Shetland had been my home base things could have been much easier. After serious consideration I came to the conclusion that enough was enough and with some regret I tendered my resignation, worked out my notice and left just before Christmas 1974.

As far as I am aware I was the first Shetlander to work offshore. This is based on the fact that I never came in contact with anyone else doing so while working on the rigs or when constantly travelling between Shetland and Aberdeen, waiting at Sumburgh Airport and at Dyce or at home on leave and being out and about speaking with folk. This now seems incredible.

The Brevik

The Brevik Hospital staff bidding farewell to sister Margaret Moar at a function in the Lerwick Hotel on 1st May 1975. *Photo by Dennis Coutts*

Back row (from left): Pearl Buckingham, Marian Young, Brian Turberville, Sonia Swannie, Susan Ollason, Elaine Campbell, Douglas Sinclair, Margaret Angus, Jessie Farmer, Lizzie Smith, Hazel Black, Baba Slater, Sandra Moar, Marlene Hill, Peter Farmer. Front row: Mary Manson, Drina Rowe, Liz Tait, Wilma Harmer, Margaret Moar, Eva Yates, Frances Corkish, Bella Thompson.

CHAPTER THREE

EPILOGUE

BACK HOME

It was great being at home over the festive period and having a relaxing, enjoyable time without having to think about returning to Aberdeen in order to join the rig. After making enquiries regarding vacancies at the Gilbert Bain Hospital I found myself starting work as a staff nurse in Ward Two on 13th January, 1975. On 9th April I was appointed Charge Nurse on night duty in the Brevik Hospital and it certainly was a good move as to my surprise and delight my take home pay was more than that of a rig medic. My spell on night duty was short lived as I replaced sister Margaret Moar on day duty when she transferred to the Maternity Unit.

Readjusting to working in a predominately female environment took some time however as I had become accustomed to hearing and then frequently using somewhat obscene American turns of phrase. When something went wrong my usual response would have been "well f*** a merry mule" but if I had slipped up and said that out loud at the Brevik it certainly would have raised more than a few eyebrows.

The hospital was a happy place in which to work and the patients were well looked after by caring staff. The building had opened as the Shetland Combination Poorhouse in 1887; was renamed Zetland County Homes in 1920 and Brevik Hospital in 1951. By the 1970s it did not meet modern standards. It closed in September 1983 when patients were moved to the new hospital at Montfield.

HEAD-HUNTED

After all the travelling in the past it was a relief to be able to walk from my home to workplace. Thoughts of what the future might hold never crossed my mind as I was settled and content working in the Brevik Hospital.

Unexpectedly one day I was asked if I would like to transfer to the nurse education department. This took me by surprise as the obvious career move would have been into nurse management. After some consideration I decided to accept the offer and was soon once again on the move. In 1976 I was seconded to work as an Unqualified Nurse Teacher at Foresterhill College, Aberdeen, prior to undertaking a Clinical Nurse Teacher course. Following qualification two years later I returned to Lerwick to fill the vacant post at the new School of Nursing based at the Gilbert Bain Hospital.

However, eight years after leaving the rig I was again head hunted when I received a call offering me the post of medic on an oil platform with a salary of more than four times my previous earnings as a medic. In addition there was the advantage of crew changing from and to Shetland.

This gave me something to seriously think about. There was no doubt I had thoroughly enjoyed my experience as a rig medic, apart from the problems associated with travelling, but since then my circumstances had dramatically changed. I was now happily married, had a gratifying job in nurse education and a busy social life. Although the prospect of earning extra money was certainly tempting I came to the conclusion that the role of an offshore medic was totally at odds with my present lifestyle. The fact that I turned down the offer was met with total astonishment.

NEW GEAR

While in Texas my purchases were mainly clothes including traditional checked shirts, flared jeans and a tie that brings back happy memories of my time there. It was later worn on occasion when attending meetings relating to NHS matters which very often turned out to be either extremely boring or controversial. After one such meeting in Aberdeen a senior nurse tutor commented that she liked the pattern on the tie and politely asked if it had a connection with Up-Helly-A'. When I turned it on its side she took one look, then shook her head and smiling said, "Oh Douglas!"

A favourite Texan tie with a pattern that is not all that it seems

A CHANGE OF DIRECTION

I continued to be employed in various roles by both Shetland Health Board and Grampian Health Board, also RGU (Robert Gordon University) until my professional working career ended with early retirement in 2001.

"When one door closes another opens" is a saying that I can identify with. I then had an opportunity to write articles about Old Lerwick for the *Shetland Life* magazine, wrote books about Lerwick and also trained as a tourist guide. This enabled me to be employed by Lerwick Port Authority for 15 years as a member of the "Meet & Greet" team who welcomed cruise ship visitors and crew to Shetland. Part of my duties was to occupy hospitality desks on board the various cruise ships that were either berthed alongside the pier or lying at anchor out in the harbour or in Breiwick. This experience allowed me once again to be out on the water and come in contact with people of all nationalities albeit in a completely different environment to that of an oil rig – but that's another story!

* 9 7 8 1 9 1 0 9 9 7 5 2 9 *

BV - #0089 - 151122 - C28 - 210/148/3 - PB - 9781910997529 - Gloss Lamination